The Big Little Peanut Butter Cookbook

The Big Little Peanut Butter Cookbook

NORMAN KOLPAS

**50 Recipes for
Delicious, Easy-to-Make
Desserts, Snacks, & Sandwiches**

CB

**CONTEMPORARY
BOOKS**

CHICAGO

Library of Congress Cataloging-in-Publication Data

Kolpas, Norman.
    The big little peanut butter cookbook / Norman Kolpas.
        p.   cm.
    Includes index.
    ISBN 0-8092-4176-5 : $6.95
    1. Cookery (Peanut butter)   I. Title.
TX814.5.P38K64   1990
641.6'413—dc20   90-39603
                                          CIP

Published by Contemporary Books, Inc.
180 North Michigan Avenue, Chicago, Illinois 60601
Manufactured in the United States of America
International Standard Book Number: 0-8092-4176-5

CONTENTS

INTRODUCTION

Peanut Butter, that quintessential all-American spread, is now more popular than ever.

According to industry statistics, we're eating record amounts of the satisfying stuff—as much as 800 million pounds of it a year, the equivalent of about three and one-third pounds for every man, woman, and child in the United States. Only about fifteen homes in a hundred fail to have a jar on hand. The Adult Peanut Butter Lovers' Fan Club, recently formed under the auspices of the Peanut Advisory Board, already boasts more than fifty thousand members. (To become a card-carrying peanut butter lover yourself, send $3.00 and a self-addressed, stamped envelope to the Adult Peanut Butter Lovers' Fan Club, P.O. Box 7528, Tifton, Georgia 31793.)

As that club's popularity might suggest, kids alone aren't responsible for all peanut butter consumption. Grown-up baby boomers, while fixing lunches and snacks for their children, have rediscovered peanut butter's simple pleasures. They've also learned that peanut butter is loaded with protein and vitamins—not to mention oils that may play a role in reducing cholesterol.

In these peanut butter-crazy times, *The Big Little Peanut Butter Cookbook* aims to serve the needs—and the tastebuds—of peanut butter lovers everywhere. Between the covers of this book are some fifty recipes for all kinds of peanut butter treats—from cookies and other baked goods to candies, from beverages to sandwich fillings familiar and unusual, from special-occasion desserts to a selection of savory recipes that show off peanut butter's attributes in a new and different light.

On the pages that immediately follow, you'll find some simple guidelines for selecting and storing peanut butter, along with instructions on how to make your own. And scattered throughout the book, you'll find special highlights from peanut butter's rich history, along with tidbits of trivia related to the spread.

Like a jar of peanut butter itself, this book is designed to be dipped into and savored time and time again. Enjoy it and let it inspire you to come up with your very own peanut butter creations.

Peanut Butter—Packing a Nutritious Punch

In these health-conscious times, one of the great discoveries people are making about peanut butter is how good it can actually be for you. The calories and nutrients it supplies make it an outstanding element of a well-balanced diet.

One of its greatest benefits is the protein it packs. Two tablespoons contain nine grams of protein, about 20 percent of a child's—and 40 percent of an adult's—daily needs. That's more protein, on an ounce-for-ounce basis, than is found in meat or cheese.

Those two tablespoons contain approximately 190 calories, about three-fourths of which come in the form of fat. While that makes peanut butter a fairly high-fat food (of some concern for people on restricted diets) the spread contains no cholesterol, and five grams' worth of fat in that two-tablespoon serving is of the polyunsaturated kind that tends to lower the levels of harmful LDL cholesterol in the bloodstream. (It's worth noting, at this point, that peanut butter appears on the lists of approved foods from both Weight Watchers® and the American Diabetes Association.)

In addition, peanut butter supplies significant quantities of a number of important vitamins and minerals. Most notably, it is a rich source of niacin, magnesium, Vitamin E, phosphorus, and copper, and it also supplies zinc, pantothenic acid, thiamin, iron, riboflavin, and calcium.

And all that at an estimated cost of just fifteen cents per serving—which makes peanut butter one delicious, nutritious bargain!

Buying Basics and Storage Tips

While most peanut butter sales are confined to a few major brands, such as Jif, Skippy, Peter Pan, and Laura Scudder's, there are literally hundreds of different brands available nationwide—most of them regional labels with devoted local followings. Far be it for this little book to dare to list or classify them all.

When making your own purchase, there are just a few basics to consider:

• Creamy or crunchy? Do you want a smooth, creamy peanut butter, or one with chunky little bits of peanuts in it? The consistency is a matter of personal preference, though a number of recipes in this book specify one type or the other.

• Seasoned or plain? It's a conventional practice for manufacturers to add salt to peanut butter, and most commercial brands contain it. But more and more, you'll find brands that give you the option of unsalted peanut butter. It's all pretty much a matter of taste and of any dietary restrictions you might be following. Some brands are sweetened with a little corn syrup or dextrose, but I always choose unsweetened varieties, which are recommended for the recipes in this book.

• Stabilized or natural? Most commercial brands today are stabilized with hydrogenated vegetable oil, which prolongs storage time by keeping the peanut butter's oil from separating out and turning rancid. So-

5

called natural or old-fashioned varieties are not stabilized; when you open them, you'll find oil floating at the top, which should be stirred back in or—if you want to cut down on the calories in your peanut butter sandwich—poured off. Once opened, these varieties require refrigeration; most stabilized brands can be kept with their lids on tight at cool cupboard temperature. I recommend using a stabilized product for the recipes in this book to obtain the most consistent results.

PEANUT BUTTER—THE REAL STUFF

In its earliest days, peanut butter was ground up in a converted meat grinder; primitive peoples still pound peanuts to a smooth paste with a mortar and pestle. Modern kitchen appliances make the task as easy as can be, and any true peanut butter lover must try—at least once—to make his or her own.

Homemade Peanut Butter

Almost everyone who really loves peanut butter has probably tried—or thought of trying—to make peanut butter. In fact, it's fairly easy to do if you have a food processor. (Electric blenders work, too, though you should cut the quantities in the recipe by half. In my experience it's much harder to clean away the last sticky traces of peanut butter in a blender.)

2 cups shelled and skinned raw peanuts
1 to 1½ tablespoons peanut oil
½ teaspoon salt (optional)

Preheat the oven to 300°F.

Spread the peanuts on a large, rimmed baking sheet. Roast them, shaking the pan every few minutes to prevent scorching, until light golden brown, 20 to 25 minutes. Remove the peanuts from the oven and pour them into a wide, heat-proof dish to cool.

Put the peanuts, oil, and if you like, the salt in a food processor fitted with the metal blade. Pulse the machine several times to chop the nuts coarsely; then process continuously until the peanut butter achieves a smooth, creamy consistency, 2 to 3 minutes, stopping a few times to scrape down the bowl with a rubber spatula. (For crunchy peanut butter, remove about ¼ cup of coarsely chopped nuts at the beginning of processing and stir them back into the finished peanut butter after it has been removed from the processor bowl.)

Scrape the peanut butter from the processor bowl into a container with an airtight lid and store it in the refrigerator. Consume it within a few weeks. If oil rises to the top of the container, stir it back in—or pour it off—before using the peanut butter.

Makes about 1 cup

Peanut Butter Sandwiches

The sandwich is the ultimate expression of individual taste in peanut butter. A filling combination that throws one peanut butter lover into a swoon of ecstasy could well cast a pall of puzzlement over someone else. To repeat a useful expression, there's no accounting for taste.

But you're sure to find a number of different sandwich ideas on the following pages that will please you in just the right way. And, likely as not, perusing them could well inspire you to come up with your own hitherto undreamt-of combinations.

Peanut Butter and Jelly

For a sandwich whose name seems to say it all, there's an almost endless number of variations on this all-American standby. You can use any number of different breads—the standard cottony white loaf or egg bread, pumpernickel or raisin bread, whole-wheat, seedless rye, sweet date-nut bread, English muffins, rice cakes, or bagels. And there's always the option of toasting the bread.

Then there's the choice of your own favorite brand of peanut butter and its style—namely, creamy or crunchy, salted or unsalted, sweetened or unsweetened. Each decision makes its own contribution to flavor and texture.

Finally, there's the jelly—or the jam, marmalade, preserves, or conserves. The classic choices seem to be grape jelly or strawberry jam. But a quick study of the offerings on any supermarket shelf opens up a wide and exciting realm of new possibilities.

I won't even begin to address the eternal debate over how the sandwich should be cut—in half or diagonally into triangles—or whether it should be left whole. And then there are those genteel souls who insist that the crusts should be trimmed.

The following basic formula delivers good results, though jam and jelly lovers may want to up the quantity of that ingredient.

2 tablespoons peanut butter
2 sandwich-sized bread slices
1 tablespoon jelly or jam

Spread the peanut butter on one side of a slice of bread. Spread the jelly on the other slice and slap the two together.

Serve with a glass of cold milk.

Serves 1

Peanut Butter and Honey

Honey, with its mellow sweetness, wonderfully complements peanut butter in sandwich fillings. If you have a sweet tooth, you may want to add a little more honey to taste.

This filling seems particularly well suited to whole-wheat bread.

2 tablespoons creamy or crunchy peanut butter
1 teaspoon honey
2 sandwich-sized bread slices

In a small bowl, stir together the peanut butter and the honey. Spread it evenly on one slice of bread and place the other on top.

Serves 1

Peanut Butter and Chocolate

As a special treat for children—or for the child in you—try this simple filling that pairs peanut butter with one of its all-time favorite companions.

Try it on a rich egg bread—French brioche is particularly good.

2 tablespoons peanut butter
2 sandwich-sized bread slices
½ tablespoon miniature semisweet chocolate chips

Spread 1 tablespoon of peanut butter on one side of each bread slice. Evenly sprinkle the chocolate chips over the peanut butter on one slice, and then place the other slice on top.

Serves 1

Peanut Butter and Banana

Banana is another filling that seems to be a natural companion to peanut butter. If you'd like the sandwich to be somewhat sweeter, drizzle a little honey over the banana.

Serve with a rich-tasting or sweet bread, such as whole-wheat, egg, pumpernickel, raisin, or date-nut.

2 tablespoons peanut butter
2 sandwich-sized bread slices
½ medium-sized ripe banana, cut into ¼-inch slices

Spread 1 tablespoon of peanut butter on one side of each bread slice. Place the banana slices evenly on top of the peanut butter on one bread slice, and place the other slice of bread on top.

Serves 1

▶ ▶ ▶ *Great Moments in Peanut Butter History #1* ◀ ◀ ◀

1890: A St. Louis physician, whose name is, sadly, lost, gets the bright idea to grind up peanuts to make an easy-to-eat protein-rich food for his toothless, elderly patients. They love it—though their tongues invariably stick to the roofs of their mouths—and peanut butter is born.

Peanut Butter and Apple

Thin slices of tart, crisp apple contrast spectacularly with peanut butter.

Serve with a rich-tasting or sweet bread, such as whole-wheat, egg, pumpernickel, raisin, or date-nut.

2 tablespoons peanut butter
2 sandwich-sized bread slices
¼ medium-sized tart, crisp apple, cored, peeled, and thinly sliced.

Spread 1 tablespoon of peanut butter on one side of each bread slice. Place the apple slices evenly on top of the peanut butter on one bread slice, and place the other slice of bread on top.

Serves 1

Peanut Butter and Raisin

A scattering of seedless raisins adds vivid contrasts of tart flavor and chewy texture to this filling. If you're a real raisin fan, you can certainly add more than the recipe calls for.

Serve on white, whole-wheat, or egg bread.

2 tablespoons peanut butter
2 sandwich-sized bread slices
1½ tablespoons seedless raisins

Spread 1 tablespoon of peanut butter on one side of each bread slice. Scatter the raisins evenly on top of the peanut butter on one bread slice, and place the other slice of bread on top.

Serves 1

☞*But Who's Counting?*

The average 12-ounce jar of peanut butter contains the equivalent of 548 peanuts.

Peanut Butter and Date

In this filling, the intense sweetness of dried dates finds a perfect foil in peanut butter.

Serve on whole-wheat, white, or egg bread.

2 tablespoons peanut butter
2 sandwich-sized bread slices
1½ tablespoons coarsely chopped dried pitted dates

Spread 1 tablespoon of peanut butter on one side of each bread slice. Scatter the dates evenly on top of the peanut butter on one bread slice, and place the other slice of bread on top.

Serves 1

Peanut Butter and Cream Cheese

For aficionados of cream cheese sandwiches, the addition of peanut butter is a revelation. For a sweeter filling, add some jam, jelly, raisins, or dates.

Serve on a sweet or rich bread, such as raisin, date-nut, or egg.

2 tablespoons peanut butter
2 sandwich-sized bread slices
1 tablespoon cream cheese, softened

Spread the peanut butter on one side of a slice of bread. Spread the cream cheese on the other side and slap the two together.

Serves 1

▶ ▶ ▶ *Great Moments in Peanut Butter History #2* ◀ ◀ ◀

1896: Joseph T. Lambert, an employee of Dr. John Harvey Kellogg and W. K. Kellogg—themselves soon to become cereal manufacturers—receives the first U.S. patent for a peanut butter machine, his adaptation of a conventional meat grinder.

Peanut Butter and Cheddar

The tang of a good, sharp cheddar cheese tastes great with peanut butter.

Serve on egg bread, whole-wheat, white, or rye.

2 tablespoons peanut butter
2 sandwich-sized bread slices
½ ounce sharp cheddar cheese, thinly sliced

Spread 1 tablespoon of peanut butter on one side of each bread slice. Distribute the cheese slices evenly on top of the peanut butter on one bread slice, and place the other slice of bread on top.

Serves 1

☞*Um, Let's Run That One Up the Flagpole . . .*

The Krema Product Company of Columbus, Ohio, launched its peanut butter in 1908 with a catchy advertising slogan from its founder, Benton Black: "I refuse to sell outside of Ohio." The company still sells peanut butter—on a regional basis, of course—to this day.

Grilled Cheese with Peanut Butter

This variation on the classic grilled cheese includes the tempting addition of crunchy peanut butter.

Make with white or egg bread.

1½ tablespoons crunchy peanut butter
2 sandwich-sized bread slices
1½ ounces sharp cheddar cheese, thinly sliced
1 tablespoon butter or margarine
1 tablespoon mayonnaise

Spread the peanut butter evenly on one side of each bread slice. Distribute the cheese slices evenly on top of the peanut butter on one bread slice, and place the other slice of bread on top.

Melt the butter or margarine over moderate heat in a skillet just big enough to hold the sandwich. Spread half the mayonnaise on one side of the sandwich, and place the sandwich in the skillet with the mayonnaise side down. Fry until golden brown. Then spread the remaining mayonnaise on the other side of the sandwich, carefully turn the sandwich over, and fry until golden brown.

Serves 1

Peanut Butter and Beefsteak Tomato

This tasty sandwich filling pairs peanut butter with a simple slice of ripe tomato. You might want to choose a salted style of peanut butter, which will highlight the tomato's flavor.

The sandwich is at its best in summer, when you can get really flavorful, firm-textured, vine-ripened beefsteak tomatoes.

Serve on plain or toasted white, whole-wheat, or egg bread.

2 tablespoons peanut butter
2 sandwich-sized bread slices
1 ¼-inch-thick slice beefsteak tomato
Freshly ground white or black pepper (optional)

Spread 1 tablespoon of peanut butter on one side of each bread slice. Place the tomato slice on top of the peanut butter on one bread slice. Season the tomato to taste with pepper, if you wish, and place the other slice of bread on top.

Serves 1

Peanut Butter and Pickle

I know this one sounds like some sort of pregnancy craving. But the salty tang of sour dill pickles actually goes very well with peanut butter. If this makes sense to you at all, give it a shot!

Serve on white, whole-wheat, or rye bread, plain or toasted.

2 tablespoons peanut butter
2 sandwich-sized bread slices
4 to 6 round dill pickle chips

Spread 1 tablespoon of peanut butter on one side of each bread slice. Distribute the pickle chips evenly on top of the peanut butter on one bread slice, and place the other slice of bread on top.

Serves 1

▶ ▶ ▶ *Great Moments in Peanut Butter History #3* ◀ ◀ ◀

1904: Some $705.11 worth of newfangled peanut butter is sold to the public from C. H. Sumner's concession stand at the St. Louis Universal Exposition.

Peanut Butter and Red Onion

Here's another combination that plays off the savory aspect of a good, salted peanut butter. If you think *this* sounds delicious, try adding a scattering of crisp crumbled bacon.

Serve on plain or toasted white, whole-wheat, rye, or pumpernickel bread.

2 tablespoons peanut butter
2 sandwich-sized bread slices
1 ¼-inch-thick slice red onion
Freshly ground white or black pepper (optional)

Spread 1 tablespoon of peanut butter on one side of each bread slice. Place the onion slice on top of the peanut butter on one bread slice. Season the onion to taste with pepper, if you wish, and place the other slice of bread on top.

Serves 1

Peanut Butter and Bacon

This is one of my all-time favorites, a perfect partnership of two rich-tasting, savory ingredients. Depending on how much salt you like—and how well your body can tolerate it—select a salted or unsalted brand of peanut butter. Crunchy or plain, it's up to you, though you'll get plenty of good, crisp texture from the bacon. If it appeals to you, add chopped scallions or a thin slice of red onion.

Try it on rye, pumpernickel, raisin, or more conventional breads, such as white, whole-wheat, or egg.

2 tablespoons peanut butter
2 sandwich-sized bread slices
2 or 3 slices bacon, cooked until crisp, drained well, and coarsely
    crumbled.

Spread 1 tablespoon of peanut butter on one side of each bread slice. Scatter the crumbled bacon on top of the peanut butter on one bread slice, and place the other slice of bread on top.

Serves 1

☞*Southern Belles*

Almost all of the peanut butter made in the United States is produced from nuts grown in Georgia, Alabama, and Florida.

Peanut Butter and Ham

If a Peanut Butter and Bacon sandwich appeals to you, this one's worth a try as well. The flavor of a good cured smoked ham wonderfully complements the nutty taste of the classic spread. If you're daring, try anointing the sandwich with a dab of Dijon-style mustard as well.

Serve on rye, pumpernickel, raisin, white, whole-wheat, or egg bread.

2 tablespoons peanut butter
2 sandwich-sized bread slices
1½ ounces thinly sliced smoked ham

Spread 1 tablespoon of peanut butter on one side of each bread slice. Arrange the ham on top of the peanut butter on one bread slice, and place the other slice of bread on top.

Serves 1

Peanut Butter Burger

I wouldn't have believed it myself a few years back, but I started seeing peanut butter as an optional topping at some of the more innovative burger eateries in my home town. Spread over a good patty of broiled beef, peanut butter does add extra-rich nuances of flavor. As with some of the other sandwich combinations, embellishments like onions and mustard are strictly optional.

6 ounces lean ground beef
Salt and freshly ground black pepper
1 whole-wheat or egg hamburger bun
½ tablespoon butter, softened (optional)
1 to 1½ tablespoons peanut butter

Preheat the broiler, grill, or barbecue.

Shape the ground beef into a round patty somewhat wider than the bun, allowing for some shrinkage during cooking. Season the patty to taste with salt and pepper and cook it close to the heat.

When the burger is almost done to your liking, split the bun and toast its cut sides alongside the burger until golden. If you like, spread them lightly with butter.

With a spatula, transfer the burger to the bottom half of the bun. Spread the top half with the peanut butter and place it on top of the burger.

Serves 1

APPETIZERS, SNACKS, AND SOUP

We're so used to thinking of peanut butter as a snack food, a sweet sandwich filling, or a dessert ingredient, that it's easy to lose sight of the fact that it's actually a flavorful ingredient. Many cultures use peanut butter in nonsweet dishes to add a rich, deep flavor and texture to all manner of foods.

Herewith, a sampling of peanut butter specialties from around the world. If they seem at all odd to you, consider throwing caution to the wind and trying just one. You might well get hooked!

The Ultimate Peanut Butter–Stuffed Celery

When I was a kid, a favorite snack was a stalk of celery smeared down its groove with a dollop of peanut butter. This more grown-up version of that basic concept makes a great snack, or an hors d'oeuvre that, because of its flavors, goes remarkably well with Bloody Marys.

¾ cup crunchy peanut butter, at room temperature
1 3-ounce package cream cheese, softened
1 tablespoon Worcestershire sauce, or to taste
A few drops Tabasco sauce, to taste
¼ cup finely chopped fresh scallion greens
1 dozen small-to-medium celery stalks, trimmed and chilled

In a mixing bowl, stir together the peanut butter, cream cheese, Worcestershire sauce, and Tabasco until smoothly blended. Fold in the scallions.

With a knife, spread a dollop of the mixture down the groove of each celery stalk. Arrange the stalks on a tray or plate and serve immediately.

Serves 6 as a snack, 12 as an hors d'oeuvre

Oniony Peanut Butter Dip

Try this rich and beguiling mixture in place of the all-time classic sour-cream-and-onion party dip. Serve with assorted chips, crackers, and raw vegetables for dipping.

2 cups sour cream
1 cup crunchy unsalted peanut butter, at room temperature
1 packet dry onion soup mix
¼ cup finely chopped fresh chives

Put the sour cream, peanut butter, onion soup mix, and half of the chives in a mixing bowl and stir with a wooden spoon or plastic spatula until thoroughly blended. (Alternatively, put them in a food processor fitted with the metal blade and pulse the machine on and off several times, just until the ingredients are combined.)

Cover the bowl and chill the dip in the refrigerator until serving time. Transfer to a serving bowl and garnish with the remaining chives.

Makes about 2¾ cups

▶ ▶ ▶ *Great Moments in Peanut Butter History #4* ◀ ◀ ◀

1922: At the Rosefield Packing Company in Alameda, California, peanut butter is churned for the first time, resulting in a smoother, creamier product.

African Cream of Peanut Butter Soup

Thoroughly contemporary in its methods and seasonings, this piquant starter nevertheless owes more than a nod of acknowledgment to traditional African soups thickened with pulverized peanuts.

2 tablespoons unsalted butter
1 medium onion, chopped fine
1 small celery stalk, chopped fine
1 small carrot, chopped fine
1 medium garlic clove, chopped fine (optional)
3 tablespoons finely chopped Italian parsley
½ cup crunchy unsalted peanut butter
1 quart chicken broth
1 cup half-and-half
½ medium tomato, stemmed, seeded, and diced

In a large saucepan, melt the butter over moderate heat. Add the onion, celery, carrot, garlic, and parsley and sauté until tender, about 5 minutes.

Reduce the heat to low and add the peanut butter, stirring continuously until it melts. Then add the broth, raise the heat slightly, and stir until the soup is smooth and begins to simmer. Continue simmering gently, stirring occasionally, for about 5 minutes more. Stir in the half-and-half and simmer briefly until heated through.

Ladle the soup into heated bowls and garnish with diced tomato.

Serves 4 to 6

☞ But How Would It Taste on Bread?

Almost six centuries ago, African tribes discovered that they could grind up a cousin of the peanut—*Voandgeia subterranea*, the Bambara groundnut—and use the paste as a thickener for their stews. The true peanut, a native of South America, was brought to West Africa in the sixteenth century by Portuguese slave traders, and it quickly supplanted the groundnut in popularity.

Indonesian Gado Gado Salad with
Warm Peanut Butter Dressing

When I first learned to make this traditional Indonesian dish, it seemed to me that instead of "Gado Gado" it should be called "Oh God! Oh God!"—so outstandingly delicious was its warm peanut butter dressing.

Present the salad, without dressing. Make the dressing just before serving and pour it from the saucepan right over the salad, tossing immediately and serving the salad while the dressing is still warm.

To serve this salad as a main course, add diced cooked chicken breast or whole small cooked shrimp. The dressing also makes a marvelous hot dip for raw vegetables. Give it a try!

Your best bet for finding shrimp paste is your local Asian market or the Asian foods section of your supermarket.

SALAD

2 cups mixed lettuces, cut into bite-sized pieces

1 cup finely shredded green cabbage

½ cup fresh bean sprouts

2 medium carrots, cut diagonally into ¼-inch-thick pieces, parboiled until tender-crisp, drained and chilled

¼ pound fresh snow peas, stemmed, stringed, parboiled until tender-crisp, drained and chilled

¼ pound whole baby button mushrooms, wiped clean (halved, if large mushrooms are used)

½ pound firm tofu (soybean curd), drained well, and cut into ½-inch cubes (optional)

2 hard-boiled eggs, chilled, shelled, and quartered

2 large scallions, thinly sliced

¼ cup finely chopped fresh cilantro leaves

WARM PEANUT BUTTER DRESSING
2 medium shallots
1 teaspoon chopped fresh ginger root
1 teaspoon shrimp paste
½ teaspoon chili powder
1 tablespoon peanut oil
1 cup crunchy peanut butter
½ cup water
2 tablespoons canned coconut cream
1 tablespoon lemon juice

For the salad, choose a large serving bowl that leaves plenty of room for tossing. Put the lettuces and cabbage on the bottom, then arrange the remaining ingredients in a decorative display, ending with a scattering of scallion and cilantro.

For the dressing, put the shallots, ginger, shrimp paste, and chili powder in a food processor fitted with the metal blade. Process until they form a smooth paste.

In a medium skillet, heat the oil over moderate heat. Add the paste from the processor and sauté for about 1 minute. Then add the peanut butter, half the water, the coconut cream, and lemon juice. Cook, stirring constantly, until the sauce reaches a simmer and is smoothly blended. Stir in enough of the remaining water to give it a thick but pourable consistency.

At the table, pour the dressing evenly over the salad. Toss and serve immediately.

Makes 6 to 8 appetizer servings

Thai Chicken Satay with Peanut Butter Dipping Sauce

Among the most appealing appetizers found on the menus of ever-more-popular Thai restaurants are these delicate kabobs of marinated chicken, served with a mildly spiced peanut butter dipping sauce. If you like, try substituting pork, lamb, beef, or even shrimp for the chicken.

Traditionally, the kabobs are cooked on thin bamboo skewers, available in most Asian markets or in the Asian food section of supermarkets. Alternatively, substitute small, thin metal skewers.

CHICKEN KABOBS
1 pound boneless, skinless chicken breasts
1 tablespoon light soy sauce
1 teaspoon honey
1 teaspoon lemon juice
½ teaspoon grated fresh ginger root
1 garlic clove, crushed

SATAY SAUCE
1 tablespoon peanut oil
2 medium shallots, chopped fine
¾ teaspoon grated fresh ginger root
Pinch of chili powder
¾ cup crunchy peanut butter
2 teaspoons light soy sauce
1 teaspoon lemon juice

With a sharp knife, carefully cut the chicken lengthwise into ¼-inch-thick and ¾-inch-wide strips. In a mixing bowl, stir together the remaining ingredients for the kabobs. Add the chicken strips, toss well, cover, and marinate in the refrigerator for about 1 hour.

If using bamboo skewers, put them in a large bowl of cold water to soak.

While the chicken is marinating, prepare the peanut sauce. In a medium saucepan, heat the peanut oil over low heat. Add the shallots and sauté just until they begin to soften, 2 to 3 minutes. Add the ginger and chili powder, sauté for about 30 seconds, and then stir in the remaining ingredients. Heat, stirring continuously, until the sauce is smooth and just begins to simmer. Set the pan aside.

Preheat the broiler or charcoal grill until very hot.

While the grill is heating, skewer the chicken strips, stitching the skewer back and forth along each strip like a needle sewing a hem. Use as many strips as needed to cover all but about ½ inch at either end of each skewer.

Grill the kabobs, turning them frequently, just until cooked through and golden, about 5 minutes depending on the heat—take care not to dry them out. Serve the kabobs accompanied by the lukewarm sauce, which should be spooned onto each individual serving plate for dipping.

Makes 6 to 8 appetizer servings

Candied Yams with Peanut Butter

Try this as a side dish at Thanksgiving, or whenever you roast a turkey or bake a ham.

6 medium yams
½ cup crunchy or smooth peanut butter
½ cup orange juice
¼ cup packed light brown sugar
2 tablespoons unsalted butter
1¼ cups miniature marshmallows

Bake the yams in a 400°F oven until soft to the touch (wear an oven mitt when you test them), about 40 minutes. Remove them from the oven.

When the yams are cool enough to handle, carefully cut them in half lengthwise. Spoon them out into a mixing bowl, reserving the shells.

With a potato masher or a fork, blend the yams with the peanut butter, orange juice, sugar, and butter. Spoon the mixture back into the shells and scatter marshmallows on top. (The yams can be prepared in advance to this stage and reserved until shortly before serving time.)

Place the filled yam halves in a shallow baking dish and return them to the 400°F oven until they are heated through and the marshmallows have partly melted and begin to turn golden, about 15 minutes.

Serves 12

FINE AND FANCY COOKIES, BROWNIES, AND BREADS

Beyond the sandwich, peanut butter's main role as an ingredient is undoubtedly in baked goods.

Anyone who loves peanut butter has, no doubt, succumbed to the pleasures of a classic, crumbly peanut butter cookie—and may well have attempted to make some at home. On the following pages, you'll find recipes for all kinds of peanut butter cookies, from the most basic, home-style varieties to the more elaborate, gourmet concoctions.

In addition, there's a selection of recipes for peanut butter brownies, muffins, tea bread, and cake—enough variety to satisfy anyone who ever feels the yearning to bake up a batch of something good.

Basic Peanut Butter Crisscross Cookies

If you're suddenly seized by the urge for a freshly baked peanut butter cookie, you can make these, ready to eat in no more than a half hour. The very basic dough is quickly mixed in a food processor and requires no chilling. The results: dense, crumbly little cookies with a good, strong taste of their featured ingredient and a traditional crisscross pattern on top.

You can easily double or even triple the recipe, the only limitation being the capacity of your processor. Likewise, you can cut the ingredients in half to make a smaller batch.

1 cup cold creamy unsalted peanut butter
1 cup all-purpose flour
1 cup granulated sugar
¼ cup margarine
1 teaspoon baking powder
½ teaspoon pure vanilla extract
½ teaspoon salt
2 medium eggs

Preheat the oven to 375°F.

Put all of the ingredients in a food processor fitted with the metal blade. Pulse the machine on and off several times, stopping once or twice to scrape down the sides of the bowl, and continue to pulse just until the ingredients are thoroughly combined and resemble coarse crumbs.

Remove the dough from the processor bowl. Scoop out a level tablespoonful of the dough and, with your hands, gently roll it into a ball. Place the ball on a nonstick or lightly greased cookie sheet. Repeat with the remaining dough, placing the balls about 2 inches apart. With a table fork, gently press down on each ball of dough to flatten it slightly, and then press down again at right angles to the first pressing to give the top a crisscross pattern. Flatten the cookies to a circle just under ½ inch thick.

Bake the cookies until their tops appear dry and lightly browned and their bottoms are golden brown, 13 to 15 minutes. With a spatula, transfer them to a wire rack to cool slightly—if you'd like them warm— or completely. Store in an airtight container.

Makes about 30

▶ ▶ ▶ *Great Moments in Peanut Butter History #5* ◀ ◀ ◀

1922-23: Joseph L. Rosefield develops and patents a method for stabilizing peanut butter by hydrogenating some of its oil, resulting in a product—packed in 1-pound tin cans—with a longer shelf life.

Peanut Butter and Jam Gems

Each of these little, bite-sized cookies is graced with a gemlike dab of jam at its center. I like strawberry jam with them—it's such a classic—but feel free to substitute your favorite flavor.

2½ cups all-purpose flour
½ tablespoon baking powder
¼ teaspoon salt
1 cup creamy peanut butter
1 cup (2 sticks) unsalted butter, softened
1 cup granulated sugar
1 cup packed light brown sugar
2 eggs
1 teaspoon vanilla
¾ cup strawberry jam, or your favorite flavor, at room temperature

In a mixing bowl, stir together the flour, baking powder, and salt. Set them aside.

In another mixing bowl, beat together the peanut butter, butter, and sugars until light and fluffy. Beat in the eggs and vanilla. Then gradually beat in the flour mixture until well combined. Cover the bowl and refrigerate for at least 1 hour.

Preheat the oven to 350°F.

Shape the dough by hand into 1-inch balls and place them about 2 inches apart on ungreased cookie sheets. With your hand, gently flatten each ball to make a circle about 1½ inches across; then press your thumb down into the center to make an indentation in each cookie.

Bake the cookies until lightly browned, 10 to 12 minutes. As soon as the cookies are out of the oven, spoon a generous ½ teaspoonful of jam into the center of each. Then carefully transfer the cookies to a wire rack to cool completely. Store in an airtight container.

Makes about 5 dozen

☞*Nuts About the Stuff*

Publicly avowed celebrity peanut butter lovers include actors Michael J. Fox, Shirley MacLaine, Jack Nicholson, Kim Basinger, Tom Selleck, and Charlton Heston; broadcasters Dan Rather and Larry King; writers George Will, William F. Buckley, Jr., and Erica Jong; athletes Brian Bosworth and Chris Evert; pop star Madonna; and ex-president Gerald Ford.

Peanut Butter and Chocolate Chip Tollbooths

These wonderfully chewy cookies, made with a rich peanut butter dough liberally dotted with semisweet chocolate chips, are not your familiar chocolate chippers.

The recipe is easily doubled or halved—but come to think of it, who on earth would want to halve it? Store any extra cookies in an airtight container at cool room temperature.

In classic fashion, serve the cookies with a tall, ice-cold glass of milk.

½ cup unsalted butter, softened
½ cup packed dark brown sugar
¼ cup light corn syrup
¼ cup creamy peanut butter
½ teaspoon pure vanilla extract
1 egg
1¼ cups all-purpose flour
½ teaspoon baking soda
¼ teaspoon baking powder
½ teaspoon salt
½ cup semisweet chocolate chips

Preheat the oven to 375°F.

In a large mixing bowl, use an electric mixer to cream the butter until fluffy. One at a time, gradually beat in the sugar, syrup, peanut butter, vanilla, and egg.

In a separate bowl, stir together the flour, baking soda, baking powder, and salt. Stirring vigorously, gradually add the dry ingredients to form a stiff batter. Fold in the chocolate chips.

44

Drop rounded teaspoonfuls of the batter about 1½ inches apart on an ungreased cookie sheet. Bake until the cookies just begin to brown lightly around the edges, about 10 minutes. Let the cookies cool slightly on the sheet, and then use a spatula to transfer them to a wire rack to cool completely.

Makes about 5 dozen

▶ ▶ ▶ *Great Moments in Peanut Butter History #6* ◀ ◀ ◀

1928: A Chicago company changes the name of its E. K. Pond brand of peanut butter to Peter Pan, named after J. M. Barrie's popular fantasy character.

Peanut Butter Shortbread

One of the all-time classic cookies—crisp and buttery—gets extra wholesomeness from the addition of peanut butter.

Store these in an airtight container. If necessary, they can be recrisped by warming them on a baking sheet in a 350°F oven for about 10 minutes.

This recipe can be doubled.

½ cup unsalted butter, softened
6 tablespoons granulated sugar
2 tablespoons packed light brown sugar
6 tablespoons creamy peanut butter
½ teaspoon pure vanilla extract
2½ cups all-purpose flour

Preheat the oven to 350°F.

In a mixing bowl, cream the butter; then beat in the sugars until the mixture looks light and fluffy. Beat in the peanut butter and vanilla until smoothly blended.

Gradually mix in just enough of the flour to make a firm but still pliant dough. Then, on a floured surface, knead the dough by hand until it is very smooth, about 10 minutes.

Press the dough into an ungreased, 8-inch square baking pan. Lightly prick its surface all over with the tines of a fork. Bake for 10 minutes at 350°F; then reduce the heat to 300°F and bake for about 40 minutes more, until lightly browned.

Remove the pan from the oven and, with a knife, deeply score the shortbread into 1″ × 4″ fingers. Let the shortbread cool in the pan completely, and then unmold it and break it carefully along the scoring marks.

Makes 16 pieces

Oatmeal–Peanut Butter Cookies

There's something very old-fashioned and wholesome about these dense, chewy cookies.

1½ cups quick-cooking rolled oats
1 cup all-purpose flour
½ cup golden seedless raisins
½ teaspoon baking powder
½ teaspoon baking soda
½ teaspoon salt
½ cup unsalted butter, softened
6 tablespoons crunchy peanut butter
1 cup packed light brown sugar
½ cup granulated sugar
1 egg
2 tablespoons water
½ teaspoon pure vanilla extract

Preheat the oven to 350°F. Lightly grease cookie sheets.

In a large mixing bowl, stir together the oatmeal, flour, raisins, baking powder, baking soda, and salt. Set aside.

In another mixing bowl, beat together the butter, peanut butter, and sugars until light and fluffy. Beat in the egg, water, and vanilla. Gradually stir the dry ingredients into the creamed mixture, stirring until thoroughly mixed.

Drop rounded teaspoonfuls of the batter about 2 inches apart on the prepared cookie sheets. Bake until golden brown, about 12 minutes. Let the cookies cool on the baking sheets for 2 or 3 minutes, and then transfer them to a rack to cool completely. Store in an airtight container.

Makes about 4 dozen

☞*Hail to the Big Three!*

About 50 percent of the country's estimated $1 billion in annual peanut butter sales is divided up by three competing national brands: Jif, Skippy, and Peter Pan.

Peanut Butter Melting Moments

Smooth and ultralight, these classic cookies benefit in both texture and taste from just a hint of you-know-what.

¾ cup (1½ sticks) unsalted butter, softened
2 tablespoons creamy peanut butter
1 teaspoon pure vanilla extract
1 cup all-purpose flour
½ cup cornstarch
½ cup confectioners' sugar
⅛ teaspoon salt

In a large mixing bowl, cream the butter until light and fluffy. Beat in the peanut butter and vanilla until smooth.

In another bowl, stir together the remaining ingredients. Then gradually beat them into the creamed mixture. Cover the bowl with plastic wrap and refrigerate for 1 hour.

Preheat the oven to 375°F.

With a spoon or a melon baller, shape the dough into balls about 1 inch in diameter and place them about 2 inches apart on an ungreased cookie sheet. With a fork or the back of a spoon, flatten them to a thickness of about ½ inch.

Bake the cookies until lightly browned, about 12 minutes. Transfer them immediately to a wire rack to cool, and then store in an airtight container.

Makes about 3 dozen

Coconut-Peanut Butter Macaroons

My favorite chewy flourless cookies get a great new flavor with the addition of peanut butter.

3 egg whites
1 cup shredded coconut
¾ cup granulated sugar
3 tablespoons peanut butter, at room temperature
1 tablespoon honey

Preheat the oven to 325°F.

In a mixing bowl, beat the egg whites until light and frothy but still fairly liquid. Add the coconut, sugar, peanut butter, and honey. With your fingers, mix the ingredients until thoroughly blended.

Drop generous teaspoonfuls of the mixture about 2 inches apart onto a greased cookie sheet. Bake until golden, about 20 minutes.

Remove the macaroons from the oven and let them cool on the baking sheet. Store in an airtight container.

Makes about 2 dozen

▶ ▶ ▶ *Great Moments in Peanut Butter History #7* ◀ ◀ ◀

1932: Joseph L. Rosefield begins producing Skippy brand peanut butter in California.

Peanut Butter Chocolate Brownies

These little cake-cookies make a wonderful after-school or lunch-box treat. Be sure to store them in an airtight container.

3 ounces unsweetened baking chocolate, coarsely chopped
¼ cup creamy peanut butter
¼ cup unsalted butter
2 eggs
½ cup granulated sugar
½ cup packed light brown sugar
1 teaspoon pure vanilla extract
1 cup all-purpose flour
1 teaspoon baking powder
¼ teaspoon salt
½ cup roasted unsalted peanuts

Preheat the oven to 350°F. Butter and flour an 8-inch square cake pan.

Fill a medium saucepan with water to about two-thirds of its depth. Bring the water to a boil and remove the pan from the heat. Place a medium heat-proof mixing bowl—just large enough to rest in the rim of the pan, with its bottom touching the water—inside the pan.

Put the chocolate, peanut butter, and butter in the bowl and stir until they have melted and blended completely. Remove the bowl from the pan and let it cool for about 15 minutes.

In a separate bowl, beat together the eggs, sugars, and vanilla until light and lemon-colored. Beating continuously, gradually pour the peanut butter–chocolate mixture into the egg mixture.

In another bowl, stir together the flour, baking powder, and salt. Gradually stir them and the peanuts into the other ingredients to make a smooth, thick batter, taking care not to overstir.

Spread the batter into the prepared pan. Bake until the top of the mixture looks dry and crusty, and the brownies yield only slightly to a careful touch, 30 to 35 minutes.

Remove the pan from the oven and place it on a wire rack. Let the brownies cool for about 15 minutes, and then cut them in the pan with a table knife into 1½-inch squares. When they have cooled completely, carefully remove them from the pan. Store in an airtight container.

Makes 2 dozen

☞*Beurre de Cacahuètes*

According to the *Dictionnaire de l'Académie des Gastronomes*, peanut butter is highly recommended as a spread for gingerbread.

Peanut Butter and Jelly Muffins

Try serving these muffins with their surprise fillings as a special treat for breakfast or lunch.

2 cups all-purpose flour
6 tablespoons granulated sugar
1½ tablespoons baking powder
½ teaspoon salt
6 tablespoons crunchy peanut butter
¾ cup milk
¼ cup (½ stick) unsalted butter, melted
1 egg, lightly beaten
¼ cup grape jelly or strawberry jam

Preheat the oven to 400°F.

In a mixing bowl, stir together the flour, sugar, baking powder, and salt. With a pastry cutter or a pair of forks, cut in the peanut butter until the mixture resembles coarse crumbs.

Add the milk, butter, and egg and stir just until combined.

Distribute the batter evenly among a dozen greased muffin cups. Spoon a scant teaspoonful of jelly or jam into the center of each cup.

Bake the muffins until golden brown, 20 to 25 minutes.

Makes 1 dozen

Peanut Butter and Date Tea Bread

Serve this wonderfully peanutty variation on traditional date-nut quick bread in generous slices, spread—of course—with your favorite jam. Feel free to use your choice of creamy or crunchy peanut butter, depending on the texture you prefer.

2 cups all-purpose flour
1 tablespoon baking powder
½ teaspoon salt
¾ cup peanut butter, at room temperature
⅓ cup honey, at room temperature
1 cup milk
1 egg, lightly beaten
¾ cup chopped dates

Preheat the oven to 350°F. Butter a 9″ × 5″ × 3″ loaf pan and set it aside.

In a mixing bowl, stir together the flour, baking powder, and salt. In a separate bowl, cream together the peanut butter and honey, and then blend in the milk and egg.

Add the moist ingredients to the dry ingredients and stir until completely blended. Then fold in the dates.

Pour the mixture into the prepared pan. Bake the bread until a wooden toothpick or thin skewer inserted into the center of the loaf comes out clean, 50 minutes to 1 hour.

Unmold the loaf and cool on a wire rack before slicing.

Makes 1 loaf

Peanut Butter–Yogurt Pound Cake

A delicious elaboration on a classic pound cake recipe, this easy dessert makes a wonderful teatime or after-dinner treat.

1 cup (2 sticks) butter, softened
2 cups granulated sugar
4 eggs
½ cup peanut butter
2½ cups all-purpose flour
½ teaspoon baking soda
1 cup plain low-fat yogurt

Preheat the oven to 350°F. Grease and flour a 10-inch tube pan.

In a mixing bowl, beat together the butter and sugar until light and fluffy. One at a time, beat in the eggs until thoroughly blended; then beat in the peanut butter.

In a separate bowl, sift together the flour and baking soda. Then gradually stir the flour mixture into the creamed mixture, alternating each addition with some of the yogurt, just until all of the ingredients are blended. Take care not to overbeat.

Pour the batter into the prepared pan and bake it until a cake tester inserted into its center comes out clean, 50 to 60 minutes.

Let the cake cool in its pan on a wire rack for about 15 minutes; then carefully unmold it and let it cool completely. Serve in thin slices.

Serves 12 to 18

RICH AND DELICIOUS
PEANUT BUTTER DESSERTS

Sometimes the occasion calls for a dessert that's really extraordinary—something that takes a little extra effort to prepare, perhaps, but yields an intensity of flavor and a marvelous texture that make the final course of the meal a truly sensuous experience.

The aim of the following peanut butter recipes is to create exceptional desserts. From an intense flourless truffle to a voluptuous mousse to ethereal soufflés, here is the crème de la crème of peanut butter creations.

You might want to try one the next time you throw a really special dinner party. Or, on the other hand, why wait? Treat your family to one of them tonight!

Giant Peanut Butter Flourless Truffle Cake

Serve this ultraelegant dessert at the end of an extra-special dinner party.

For the chocolate, choose an imported bittersweet variety with a high cocoa butter content, such as Tobler's Tobamera, Caraque from Valrhona, or Lindt—available in gourmet stores.

10 ounces bittersweet chocolate, broken into pieces
¼ cup creamy peanut butter
½ cup heavy cream
2 tablespoons cognac (optional)
¼ cup chopped peanuts
½ cup whipping cream

Fill a medium saucepan with water to about two thirds of its depth. Bring the water to a boil and remove the pan from the heat. Place a medium heat-proof mixing bowl—just large enough to rest in the rim of the pan, with its bottom touching the water—inside the pan.

Put the chocolate and peanut butter in the bowl. Stir with a wire whisk until they are completely melted and smoothly blended. Leave the bowl resting inside the pan.

Put the cream in a small saucepan over low heat and heat it until bubbles begin to form around its edge.

Whisking the chocolate continuously, slowly pour the hot cream into the bowl, continuing to whisk until it is completely blended. Then, if you wish, whisk in the cognac.

Line a shallow, 8-inch round cake pan with waxed paper. Pour the truffle mixture into the pan and spread it smoothly and evenly. Cover the pan with plastic wrap and refrigerate it for several hours or overnight, until firmly chilled.

Before serving, unmold the truffle onto a round platter. Peel off the waxed paper. With your hand, gently press the chopped peanuts into the edge of the truffle all the way around its circumference.

Whip the whipping cream just until it forms soft peaks.

With a sharp knife, cut the truffle into thin wedges and transfer each wedge to a serving plate. Garnish with whipped cream.

Serves 12

☞ *Dare We Call It Peanut Buttergate?*

During the Nixon administration, urban redevelopment not far from 1600 Pennsylvania Avenue led to an infestation of rats in the White House. The solution: traps baited with peanut butter disposed of the vermin in next to no time.

Frozen Peanut Butter–Cream Cheese Pie

Like a frozen cheesecake, this old-fashioned dessert has a rich, satisfying tang. Let it sit at room temperature for about 15 minutes before cutting and serving it in thin slices.

1 8-ounce package cream cheese, at room temperature
1 cup confectioners' sugar
½ cup creamy peanut butter, at room temperature
½ cup sour cream
1 teaspoon pure vanilla extract
1 cup whipping cream, whipped to soft peaks
1 prepared 9-inch graham cracker crust
2 ounces semisweet chocolate, carefully cut into thin shavings with a
    vegetable peeler

In a mixing bowl, beat the cream cheese with the sugar until light and fluffy. Beat in the peanut butter, then the sour cream, and then the vanilla. With a rubber spatula, gently fold in the whipped cream, just until blended.

Spread the filling on the graham cracker crust and garnish its surface with chocolate shavings. Freeze until firm, at least 3 hours. Serve in thin slices.

Serves 12

Peanut Butter and Jam Bread Pudding

One of the all-time-favorite old-fashioned desserts becomes even more satisfying through the addition of peanut butter and jam.

Start with bread that's a day or two old and slightly dry and firm.

8 slices egg bread
¼ cup peanut butter
¼ cup raspberry jam, or your favorite flavor
3 eggs
½ cup granulated sugar
2 cups milk
½ cup whipping cream

Preheat the oven to 350°F.

Spread one side of the bread with peanut butter, and then jam. Cut the slices into thirds and layer them spread-sides-up evenly in a buttered, 1½-quart baking dish, ending with a layer of slices plain-side-up.

In a mixing bowl, lightly beat the eggs. Stir in the sugar, and then whisk in the milk until blended. Pour the mixture evenly over the layered bread slices and let them sit for about 15 minutes.

Put the pudding in the oven and bake until the top is golden brown and a small, sharp knife inserted into the center comes out clean, about 45 minutes.

Remove the pudding from the oven. Whip the cream until soft peaks form. Serve the pudding warm, spooned into shallow bowls and garnished with whipped cream.

Serves 6 to 8

Peanut Butter Soufflés with Cinnamon Whipped Cream

Serve this dessert as an ending to a really glamorous dinner. Although the procedure is somewhat involved, you'll be surprised by how easy it really is to make.

SOUFFLE CUP PREPARATION
Butter, softened, for soufflé dishes
Granulated sugar, for soufflé dishes

SOUFFLE MIXTURE
6 tablespoons unsalted butter
6 tablespoons all-purpose flour
1¾ cups milk
6 large egg yolks
½ cup granulated sugar
½ cup plus 2 tablespoons creamy peanut butter
12 egg whites
Pinch of salt

CINNAMON WHIPPED CREAM
1½ cups whipping cream, chilled
1 tablespoon confectioners' sugar
½ teaspoon ground cinnamon
¼ teaspoon pure vanilla extract

Preheat the oven to 450°F. Generously butter the insides of 8 individual 10-ounce ceramic soufflé dishes or baking cups. Sprinkle granulated sugar inside each dish, turning the cup to coat the butter evenly, and then shaking out the excess.

In a medium saucepan, melt the 6 tablespoons of butter over low heat. Add the flour and cook, stirring with a wire whisk, for about 3 minutes, taking care not to let the flour brown.

With the whisk, gradually stir in the milk. Stirring continuously, let the mixture come to a simmer, and then remove it from the heat.

In a mixing bowl, beat the egg yolks with half of the sugar until creamy and lemon-colored. Whisking continuously, slowly pour about 1 cup of the warm milk mixture into the egg mixture. Then pour the contents of the bowl back into the saucepan and continue cooking over low heat, whisking continuously, until the mixture is very thick, about 2 minutes. Remove the pan from the heat and stir in the peanut butter until well blended. Pour the mixture through a sieve into a heat-proof bowl, pressing it through with a wooden spoon.

In a clean mixing bowl, beat the egg whites with the salt until they form soft peaks. Then, still beating, gradually add the remaining sugar and continue beating until stiff, shiny peaks form.

With a rubber spatula, stir about a third of the egg whites into the peanut butter base to lighten it. Then gently fold in the remaining egg whites.

Spoon the soufflé mixture into the prepared baking cups. Bake until risen and golden brown, 18 to 20 minutes.

While the soufflés are baking, prepare the whipped cream. Put the cream in a mixing bowl and beat just until it begins to thicken. Then add the sugar, cinnamon, and vanilla and continue beating until it forms soft peaks.

Carefully transfer each soufflé to an individual heat-proof serving dish. Pass the whipped cream to be spooned generously onto the center of each soufflé.

Serves 8

Chocolate–Peanut Butter Mousse

We're all familiar with chocolate mousse. Here's a peanutty variation on that smooth, creamy, airy concoction.

½ pound semisweet baking chocolate, broken into pieces
¼ cup milk
¼ cup (½ stick) unsalted butter, softened
3 tablespoons creamy peanut butter
3 tablespoons granulated sugar
4 large eggs, yolks and whites separated
½ cup whipping cream, whipped to soft peaks

Put the chocolate, milk, butter, and peanut butter in a medium-heavy saucepan over low heat. When the chocolate begins to melt, remove the pan from the heat and stir until the mixture is smooth.

In a mixing bowl, beat the sugar together with the egg yolks until light and lemon-colored. Then, with a wooden spoon, gradually beat the egg yolk mixture into the chocolate mixture in the pan.

In a separate, clean bowl, beat the egg whites until they form stiff peaks. Stir about a quarter of the egg whites into the saucepan; then, with a rubber spatula, gently fold the contents of the pan into the remaining egg whites in the bowl. Finally, fold in the whipped cream.

Empty the bowl into a deep, 1½-quart serving dish. Cover and refrigerate for at least 3 hours or overnight. To serve, spoon into individual chilled dishes.

Serves 6 to 8

ICE CREAMS AND SAUCES

Ice cream lovers are as devoted to their favorite dessert as peanut butter lovers are to their favorite spread. Combine the two in a single recipe, and you've got something custom-made to excite the passions.

The recipes that follow aim to capture the essence of both loves in a single scoop—or a double or triple, if you're so inclined. There's an ice cream version of peanut butter's classic pairing with jelly and two frozen treats that imaginatively combine peanut butter with chocolate. And for those who like to add extra embellishment to their desserts, there's a hot fudge sauce that will turn any flavor of ice cream into a peanut butter sensation.

If you really want to go wild, make up batches of all the recipes in this chapter, and treat your family and friends to a peanut butter-ice cream party. Be sure to supply assorted appropriate garnishes, such as chopped peanuts, Reese's pieces and peanut butter chips. After all: What's the point of doing it if you're not going to be excessive about it?

▶ ▶ ▶ *Great Moments in Peanut Butter History #8* ◀ ◀ ◀

1940-45: With tin in short supply, peanut butter manufacturers begin to pack their products in glass jars. Peanut butter is supplied to soldiers abroad as a popular ration.

Peanut Butter and White Chocolate Ice Cream

If you own an ice cream maker of any sort—whether hand-cranked or electric—you can mix and enjoy this sublime ice cream in next to no time.

2 eggs
1 egg yolk
⅔ cup granulated sugar
¾ cup crunchy peanut butter, at room temperature
½ teaspoon pure vanilla extract
1 quart half-and-half
¾ cup white chocolate chips

In a mixing bowl, beat the eggs, egg yolk, and sugar until light and frothy. Beat in the peanut butter and vanilla until smoothly blended. Then stir in the half-and-half.

Freeze the mixture in an ice cream freezer, following the manufacturer's instructions. When the ice cream begins to thicken but is still not yet solid, add the white chocolate chips—letting the paddles of the machine stir them into the mixture. Continue freezing until the ice cream is solid.

Serve immediately; or store the ice cream in the freezer in a covered container, letting it soften at room temperature for 15 to 30 minutes before scooping and serving.

Makes about 1½ quarts

Peanut Butter and Jelly Ice Cream

For this variation on the mixture that forms the base for Peanut Butter and White-Chocolate Ice Cream, I like to use grape jelly—to me, the definitive companion to peanut butter in the time-honored lunch-box sandwich.

2 eggs
1 egg yolk
⅔ cup granulated sugar
¾ cup crunchy peanut butter, at room temperature
½ teaspoon pure vanilla extract
1 quart half-and-half
¾ cup grape jelly, at room temperature

In a mixing bowl, beat the eggs, egg yolk, and sugar until light and frothy. Beat in the peanut butter and vanilla until smoothly blended. Then stir in the half-and-half.

Freeze the mixture in an ice cream freezer, following the manufacturer's instructions. Just before the ice cream is done, add the jelly to the freezer container, letting the paddles of the machine turn a few revolutions more to stir it into the mixture.

Serve immediately; or store the ice cream in the freezer in a covered container, letting it soften at room temperature for 15 to 30 minutes before scooping and serving.

Makes about 1½ quarts

Chocolate Fudge Ice Cream with Peanut Butter Swirl

It's one of the hottest varieties in ice cream today—a rich chocolate ice cream shot through with a thick ribbon of peanut butter. I find that using a salted brand of peanut butter adds an intriguing edge to the taste.

2½ cups half-and-half
2 ounces unsweetened chocolate
2 egg yolks
1 whole egg
½ cup granulated sugar
¼ cup plus 2 tablespoons light corn syrup
1 teaspoon pure vanilla extract
¾ cup creamy peanut butter

In a heavy saucepan, heat the half-and-half with the chocolate over low heat, stirring constantly until the chocolate melts completely and blends with the half-and-half. Remove the pan from the heat. Pour its contents into a heat-proof bowl and put the bowl in the freezer to chill while you prepare the other ingredients.

In a mixing bowl, beat the egg yolks, egg, and sugar until light and frothy. Beat in all but 2 tablespoons of the corn syrup, and then beat in the vanilla until smoothly blended. Then gradually whisk in the half-and-half and chocolate mixture.

Freeze the mixture in an ice cream freezer, following the manufacturer's instructions. When the ice cream just begins to thicken, put the peanut butter and the remaining corn syrup in a medium saucepan over low heat and stir until the peanut butter melts. Just before the ice cream is done, pour in the peanut butter, letting the paddles of the machine turn a few revolutions more to stir it into the mixture.

Serve immediately; or store the ice cream in the freezer in a covered container, letting it soften at room temperature for 15 to 30 minutes before scooping and serving.

Makes about 1½ quarts

▶ ▶ ▶ *Great Moments in Peanut Butter History #9* ◀ ◀ ◀
1958: Procter & Gamble introduces Jif brand peanut butter.

Hot Peanut Butter–Fudge Sauce

Simmer up a quick batch of this easy topping and pour it over your favorite flavor of ice cream for a real peanut butter lover's sundae. If you like, you can top it off with a scattering of roasted peanuts, Reese's pieces, M&M's, or some other favorite embellishment.

While it may seem a somewhat futile gesture, you can substitute low-fat or nonfat evaporated milk in this recipe—with good results.

Any leftover sauce may be stored in a covered container in the refrigerator for several days. Rewarm the sauce over very gentle heat before serving.

1 cup evaporated milk
1 cup creamy or crunchy peanut butter
½ cup packed dark brown sugar
½ cup granulated sugar
½ cup honey

Put all of the ingredients in a heavy saucepan. Stir over low heat until the sugars have dissolved, the peanut butter has melted, and all of the ingredients are smoothly blended.

Raise the heat slightly and, still stirring, bring the mixture to a brisk simmer. Continue simmering for 5 minutes, stirring and scraping the bottom and sides of the pan continuously.

Spoon the sauce immediately over scoops of ice cream, or keep it warm over a bowl of hot water until ready to serve.

Makes about 2 cups, enough for 8 to 12 scoops of ice cream.

CONFECTIONS AND BEVERAGES

Peanut butter has such a voluptuous texture and taste that it's a natural in candies. In its way, it's every bit as appealing and satisfying as chocolate.

On the following pages, you'll find peanut butter playing a starring—or major supporting—role in a number of sweet confections. Fudge figures prominently here, resembling, as it does, peanut butter's natural consistency. There's also a recipe for a gourmet variation on popular style of peanut butter candy, along with a couple of recipes for really old-fashioned treats.

As a bonus, three recipes are included for drinks that feature peanut butter—from fountain-style concoctions to a simple, comforting hot drink that could take the place of your favorite evening cup of cocoa.

Chocolate–Peanut Butter Fudge

This firm, meltingly delicious fudge perfectly blends two classic confectionery flavors. Use creamy or chunky peanut butter—whichever you prefer.

2 cups granulated sugar
½ cup milk
2 tablespoons light corn syrup
1 tablespoon unsalted butter
¼ pound semisweet chocolate, chopped fine or grated
6 tablespoons peanut butter
1 teaspoon pure vanilla extract

Lightly coat an 8-inch square baking pan with flavorless oil or a non-stick spray.

In a large, heavy saucepan, stir together the sugar, milk, and corn syrup until thoroughly blended. Add the butter and chocolate, put the pan over low heat, and continue stirring until the sugar dissolves and the chocolate melts.

Raise the heat to moderate and, still stirring continuously, bring the mixture to a boil. Continue boiling, undisturbed, for about 5 minutes, until the mixture reaches 234°F on a candy thermometer—or forms a soft ball when a small spoonful is submerged in ice water.

Remove the pan from the heat and let it cool at room temperature, without stirring, until lukewarm—about 110°F. Then add the peanut butter and vanilla and stir vigorously until they are thoroughly blended and the mixture is thick.

Spread the fudge evenly in the prepared cake pan and let it cool completely. Then cut it into 1-inch squares and remove them from the pan. Store any leftover fudge in layers, separated by waxed paper, in an airtight container kept in a cool place.

Makes 64 pieces, about 1½ pounds

Cream Cheese and Peanut Butter Fudge

Amazingly quick to make, this ultrasmooth fudge pairs the richness of cream cheese with the distinctive taste and texture of crunchy peanut butter.

1 3-ounce package cream cheese
3 tablespoons crunchy peanut butter
½ teaspoon pure vanilla extract
2 cups confectioners' sugar

In a mixing bowl, beat the cream cheese with the peanut butter and vanilla until smooth. Gradually beat in the sugar.

Press the mixture evenly into the bottom of a buttered 9″ × 5″ loaf pan. Refrigerate for at least 2 hours, until the fudge is firm. Then unmold and cut into 1-inch squares.

Makes 45 pieces, about 1 pound

Exalted Peanut Butter Cups

Prepared from imported bittersweet chocolate, and with a peanut butter filling sweetened ever so slightly with honey, these confections of generous size exceed the expectations of the most devout candy lovers. And if you're like me, you'll prefer to eat them after they have been chilled in the refrigerator, or even frozen. (But, if you do so, be careful of any problem teeth you might have!)

For the chocolate, choose an imported bittersweet variety with a high cocoa butter content, such as Tobler's Tobamera, Caraque from Valrhona, or Lindt—available in gourmet stores.

1¾ pounds imported bittersweet chocolate, broken into pieces
1½ cups chunky peanut butter
¼ cup honey

Fill two medium saucepans with water to about two-thirds of their depth. Bring the water to a boil and remove the pans from the heat. Place a medium-sized heat-proof mixing bowl—just large enough to rest in the rim of the pan, with its bottom touching the water—inside each pan.

Put the chocolate in one bowl and the peanut butter and honey in the other. Stir the contents of each bowl until completely melted and smooth.

Place two dozen shallow waxed-paper candy cups with diameters of about 2½ inches—or the same number of similar sized cupcake cups—in muffin tins. Pour 1 tablespoon of the chocolate into the bottom of each cup. Put the muffin tins in the refrigerator to chill the chocolate in the cups just until it has solidified, about 10 minutes. Remove the muffin tins and top the chocolate in each cup with 1 good tablespoonful of the peanut butter mixture; return the tins to the refrigerator until that layer has set. Then repeat the procedure with the remaining chocolate, sealing in the peanut butter layer in each cup.

Refrigerate for about 2 hours before serving. Store any remaining candies in an airtight container kept in a cool place.

Makes about 2 dozen

▶ ▶ ▶ *Great Moments in Peanut Butter History #10* ◀ ◀ ◀

1990: Peanut butter celebrates its 100th anniversary—a year that sees America's love of the stuff flourishing as never before, with more than 50 million people enjoying the spread in some form every day.

Peanut Butter and Chocolate Chip Meringues

The joy of a good meringue is the way it just melts in the mouth, virtually disappearing but leaving behind its wonderful flavor. These are the lightest peanut butter cookies imaginable.

2 large egg whites
½ teaspoon pure vanilla extract
⅛ teaspoon cream of tartar
Pinch of salt
⅔ cup granulated sugar
6 tablespoons creamy peanut butter, at room temperature
3 tablespoons miniature semisweet chocolate chips

Preheat the oven to 300°F.

In a mixing bowl, beat the egg whites with the vanilla, cream of tartar, and salt until they form soft peaks. Little by little, beat in the sugar; when it has all been incorporated, continue beating just until the whites form stiff and shiny—but not dry—peaks.

Gently fold in the peanut butter and chocolate chips just until combined.

Drop the mixture in generous teaspoonfuls, about 1½ inches apart, onto a greased cookie sheet. Bake until lightly browned, about 25 minutes. With a spatula, immediately remove the meringues from the cookie sheet onto a wire rack to cool.

Store in an airtight container.

Makes about 3 dozen

Peanut Butter Popcorn Balls

These old-fashioned confections make a great after-school treat or evening snack. I prefer to make them with air-popped corn, but you can pop the corn in a conventional stove-top popper if you wish.

¾ cup light corn syrup
¼ cup granulated sugar
2 tablespoons packed light brown sugar
1 cup creamy peanut butter
3 quarts popped popcorn
¾ cup whole roasted skinless peanuts
¾ cup shredded coconut

In a medium saucepan, stir the corn syrup and sugars over moderate heat until the sugars dissolve and the mixture comes to a boil.

Remove the pan from the heat and stir in the peanut butter until it melts.

Put the popcorn in a large mixing bowl. Pour the peanut butter mixture evenly over it, and then sprinkle the peanuts and coconut on top. With a wooden spoon, stir the mixture until the dry ingredients are evenly coated and thoroughly combined.

As soon as the mixture is cool enough to handle, grease your hands and shape it into a dozen generous balls. Eat immediately, or wrap the balls in waxed paper and store them in an airtight container.

Makes 12

Malted Peanut Butter and Banana Smoothie

Thick, smooth, and creamy in its consistency, this healthful shake is a great drink for starting off the day. It also makes a terrific afternoon or after-school snack. If you like, you can substitute low-fat or nonfat milk for the whole milk.

The ice cubes produce a frostier and—because they take longer to blend in—a frothier result. If you prefer your smoothie less airy, omit the ice.

1 cup cold milk
2 tablespoons creamy peanut butter
2 teaspoons honey
2 teaspoons malt powder
1 small-to-medium fully ripened banana
2 ice cubes (optional)

Put all of the ingredients in an electric blender. Blend at medium speed until they are smoothly combined. Serve immediately in a tall glass.

Serves 1

Peanut Butter Shake

A good spoonful of peanut butter will transform your favorite milk-shake into an extra-rich taste sensation. In my favorite version, the peanut butter is added to a traditional chocolate shake.

¾ cup chilled milk
1 scoop (¼ cup) rich vanilla ice cream
2 tablespoons chocolate syrup
1 tablespoon creamy peanut butter

Put all of the ingredients in an electric blender. Blend at medium speed until they are smoothly combined. Serve immediately in a tall chilled glass.

Serves 1

☞*Tomorrow the Soviets?*

While peanut butter lovers are almost exclusively confined to America, their ranks are growing in other parts of the world. Consumption is on the rise in such nations as Great Britain, Canada, and Saudi Arabia, and U.S. peanut exports are approaching the 1-billion-pound mark.

Hot Peanut Butter Milk

Sipped from a large, heavy mug, this soothing beverage is wonderful on a chilly evening.

¾ cup milk
1 tablespoon peanut butter
1 to 2 tablespoons honey
Ground cinnamon or grated nutmeg

In a small saucepan, heat the milk with the peanut butter over low heat, stirring continuously. When the milk is hot and the peanut butter has melted and blended with it completely, stir in the honey to taste.

Remove the pan from the heat. With a small whisk, briskly stir the milk to form a light froth. Pour the milk into a large, heated mug and lightly dust with cinnamon or nutmeg before serving.

Serves 1

INDEX